The Changing Seasons

Spring

Paul Humphrey

W

FRANKLIN WATTS
LONDON•SYDNEY

This edition 2012

Franklin Watts
338 Euston Road
London NW1 3BH

Franklin Watts Australia
Level 17/207 Kent Street
Sydney, NSW 2000

A CIP catalogue record for this book is available from the British Library

Dewey classification number: 578.4'3

ISBN: 978 1 4451 0712 7

Planning and production by Discovery Books Limited
Editors: Paul Humphrey, Rebecca Hunter
Designer: Jemima Lumley

Photo credits: CFW Images/Chris Fairclough: 8, 10, 11, 12, 13, 19, 25; CFW Images/EASI-Images: 5, 20 and front cover (Ed Parker), 16 (Neal Cavalier-Smith); Chris Fairclough: 28, 29; FLPA: 15 (Martin B Withers), 22 (Nigel Cattlin); Getty Images: 6 (David Paterson), 9 (Bob Herger), 17 (Bob Elsdale), 18 (John Francis-Blake), 27 (John Giustina); Istockphoto.com: back cover (Debi Gardiner), 14 (Rob Friedman), title page and 21 (Svetlana Prikhodkc), 23 (Jim Jurica), 24 (Gord Horne), 26.

Printed in China

Franklin Watts is a division of Hachette Children's Books, an Hachette UK company.
www.hachette.co.uk

Contents

Spring starts   6

First flowers   8

Animals are born   10

Buds and leaves   12

Birds nesting   14

Being outside   16

Sun and rain   18

Blossom and bees   20

Tadpoles and baby birds   22

On the farm   24

Summer is coming!   26

Spring projects   28

Index   30

Spring is the season that follows winter.

The weather can still be cold
at the beginning of spring.

Crocuses are the first garden flowers to appear in spring.

They are followed
later by daffodils.

In spring, young animals are born ...

... and frogspawn
appears in ponds.

Buds on the trees get fatter.

Soon the leaves
begin to grow.

Birds collect grass and twigs to build a nest.

Soon they are busy
feeding baby birds.

By the middle of spring, the evenings are lighter.

People enjoy
being outside.

17

Spring weather can be warm and sunny.

But it can be wet and
windy sometimes too!

The trees are full of blossom.

The bees collect
nectar from flowers.

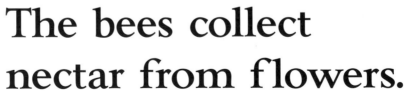

Later in spring, the frogspawn turns into tadpoles.

Baby birds are
hungry. Soon they
will learn to fly.

In the farmer's field, the crops are growing.

Sheep enjoy
the spring
grass.

By the end of spring, the weather is warmer.

We can play outside.
Summer is coming!

Spring projects

Collect sticky buds

Buds start to get fatter on the trees in early spring.
By the end of spring, leaves have appeared.

You will need:
A variety of different twig cuttings with buds on
One or two vases of water ✽ Some labels

What to do:

1. Tie a label to each twig cutting with the name of the tree it came from, if you know what it is.

2. Place the different twig cuttings into the vases of water.

3. Watch to see which buds open out into leaves first.

4. Try to identify the trees from their leaves.

Coloured flowers

In the spring, plants need lots of water to help them grow.
You can see how this works and make a colourful flower
at the same time.

You will need:
A white daisy or carnation
A glass with about 2.5 cm of water ✿ Some food colouring

What to do:
1. Add a tablespoon of food
colouring to the water in the glass.

2. Put the flower in the water and
leave for 24 hours.

3. The petals of the flower will start to
change colour. This is because the
flower is taking in the coloured water
up its stem.

Index

Animals   10

Bees   21
Birds   14-15, 23
Blossom   20
Buds   12-13, 28

Cows   10
Crocuses   8
Crops   24

Daffodils   9

Farming   24-25
Flowers   8-9, 21, 29
Frogspawn   11, 22

Leaves   13, 28

Nectar   21
Nests   14-15

Rain   19

Sheep   24-25
Summer   27

Tadpoles   22
Trees   6-7, 20

Weather   7, 18-19, 26
Wind   19
Winter   6